M000195834

Marco Lemessi

SERVE to lead

ISBN 978-1-7352054-5-8

Cover by *Les, germancreative*

To my Mother,
Role Model of Servant Leader

To Rainer & Gordon,
Supervisors, Mentors, Friends

"Your employees come first. And if you treat your employees right, guess what? Your customers come back, and that makes your shareholders happy. Start with employees and the rest follows from that."

Herb Kelleher, Cofounder of Southwest Airlines

CONTENTS

FOREWORD

Dr. Marco Lemessi and I apparently have a few things in common.

Starting from the obvious ones, we're both Italians. We're actually both from central Rome, and we're both AS Roma supporters. We're both part of the so-called Gen X. In fact, we were both born in 1972. Both in December. To be precise, both on the 2nd of December (what a coincidence, uh?). We have been classmates for 8 years, from the first day of our 6th grade to the day we got our High School Diploma.

We both left Rome, and Italy, for work. And we both had a rather successful career far from home, associating our names to top tier multinational companies and... keeping ourselves as far as possible from the "*Veni, Vidi, Vici*" approach that our fellow citizen Julius Caesar had implemented many years before! On the contrary, both of us have been trying our best to learn and understand the different cultural backgrounds, work ethics, values, sensitivities and points of view of the people we had to manage (and the ones we were managed by), in order to better work with them.

Did we do this because we are nice individuals? Sure, it all came natural to both of us, despite some inevitable challenges. But you don't need to be a genius to understand that your diverse, multicultural teams will respond much better if you, as their manager, show empathy, respect, genuine interest in their professional and personal growth, and start inspiring and mentoring them even before managing them. In order to be a leader, you need to have followers. If you run a 100-people team and these 100 people don't really follow you but just execute your orders—or even pretend to—you are not a leader. You are nothing more than a bad manager. Try to inspire your teams instead, share some relevant information with them, make them feel part of a bigger thing, instill purpose, encourage them, show them trust and support, praise them in public for their successes… and you shouldn't be surprised if they will feel engaged and often overperform.

Now, let's go back to our school days.

I was a rather good student. Among the top 5 in my class, or maybe top 7, depending on the subject, on the teacher, on the term and on my motivation. That is where the main difference with Marco was. He was always the top student: n. 1 in Italian, in Latin, in

Greek, in History, Geography, Philosophy, English, Math, Science, you name it.

Could I ever imagine, back then, that one day Marco would become a leader?

Yes, I knew he would become a good leader.

And let me be clear: as a kid, I didn't like top performers. I was suspicious. How could I trust someone who would never fail, someone who would always look good in front of the teacher (any teacher!)? Someone who would seem to stand on the teachers' side, and thus against the other students?

Marco was different, though. He would keep earning his well-deserved high marks and complain when someone wanted to copy from his notebook without even making the effort to understand what the problem to be solved was; but on "war days" (oral or written tests) he would never for a second forget he was on the students' side, and would always help school friends struggling with a Latin translation test or a hard geometry problem.

What does that all mean?

1) Marco had personality and an iron will. He was not a robot, he was a teenager like the rest of us. And he must have thought "I don't feel like studying

today", at least once. But if that ever occurred to him, that lazy temptation was certainly short-lived.

2) Marco had confidence. He knew he was ready to study as hard as it takes to be the n. 1 student throughout the school years and afterwards, and he knew he would succeed.

3) Marco was generous. Let's be fair: when you study very hard for a test, you aren't necessarily happy to prompt all the right answers to somebody who's been studying much less...

I didn't know, back in the 1980s, that Marco would become a great engineer. He could have ended up becoming a great surgeon, or a great astronaut. But I had no doubt he was going to be a good leader. Someone who would steer the ship while also supporting his crew in doing the rowing, someone definitely leading by example, with empathy and with kindness.

By the way, Marco would never admit it, but I suspect he asked me to write this foreword not because it's beneficial to his book, but because he thought it could help me get additional exposure and ideally land new business!

Francesco Denti

AUTHOR'S NOTE

When referring to a non-specific gender (e.g., *manager*, *leader*, *team member*), there seems to be no clear rule on which pronoun to use ("he/she", "he or she", "he", "she").

The unspoken rule in the past was to use masculine pronouns when referring to a non-specific gender. In today's equal-opportunity world, both male and female pronouns are widely used when the gender is not specified.

This book follows Jane Friedman's suggestion [Friedman, 2010]: alternating pronouns. If in one example masculine pronouns are used to refer to a non-specific gender, in the example that follows the pronouns are feminine.

This avoids the clunkiness of writing all the time "his or her" or "his/her" and it does not hurt—we hope—anyone's feelings.

INTRODUCTION

The day when my professional life started has an exact date: February 19th, 1998. The day when I discussed my Master Thesis in Engineering in the grandiose scenery of the 15-century cloister of *San Pietro in Vincoli*[1], only a few hundred meters away from the Colosseum, in the heart of Rome. The day when the student officially became the engineer.

Over the following two decades, my professional career has taken me all around the globe and made me—also—a frequent flyer with several airlines. I have been given the opportunity to learn foreign languages, get in touch with different cultures, experience diverse perspectives, develop new skills, and eventually grow into the person I am today.

I lived and worked in different countries, visited countless places around the world, and teamed up with people from dozens of different nations.

Inspired by the principles of Servant Leadership—which will be briefly discussed in the next chapter—this book showcases my own vision of leadership, and

---

[1] St. Peter in Chains.

is based on personal experiences I made, stories I heard from colleagues, classmates and friends, and lessons I learned in my career.

Every career is made of peaks and valleys, successes and failures. In the pages that follow I will share with you what worked for me, and what did not—and why. Failures are not necessarily a bad thing if they make you learn, grow and evolve.

Over the past twenty years I had the opportunity to work for many different managers. I am using the word *manager* instead of *leader* on purpose here, and I will discuss this topic in more details in the next chapter.

What I would like to point out here is that I learned valuable lessons from each one of them, without exception. Some of them taught me how a leader acts. Others taught me—unintentionally—how a leader should **not** act. I am grateful to both groups.

> *"There is plenty to be learned even from a bad teacher: what not to do, how not to be."*
> **J. K. Rowling**, Author

SERVANT LEADERSHIP

The Servant as Leader

Back in 2015, during one of my business visits to the United States, I was introduced to the fundamentals of **Servant Leadership**. I had heard of Servant Leadership before, and I dug deeper into it later, especially during my studies at Frankfurt School of Finance & Management. However, it was that 2015 class in the US the real game-changer in my leadership style.

The phrase *servant leadership* was coined by Robert K. Greenleaf in his essay *The Servant as Leader* [Greenleaf, 1970].

> *"He who does not live to serve is not useful for living"* [*"Non serve per vivere chi non vive per servire"*].
> **Jorge Mario Bergoglio**, Pope & Bishop of Rome

Servant Leadership is a philosophy and set of practices that turns the tables on the relationship between the leader and those being led. *"A servant-leader focuses primarily on the growth and well-being of people and the communities to which they belong. While traditional leadership generally involves the accumulation and exercise of power by one at the 'top of the pyramid', servant leadership is different. The servant-leader shares power, puts the needs of others first and helps people develop and perform as highly as possible"* [RKGC, 2020].

Servant leadership is not merely benevolent management or—worse—lack of management. Servant leaders are usually very demanding of their teams, they demand their people to use their talents to the fullest. Servant leaders set high standards for themselves and those around them.

What differentiates servant leaders from traditional managers are their *focus* and their *perspective*:

- Their **focus** is on *what* needs to be done, not *how* things get done. Servant leaders concentrate on the growth of their people, on making them more autonomous by inspiring and empowering them.

- Their **perspective** is to serve their employees rather than being served by them.

Leadership vs. Management

A lot has been written on the difference between managers and leaders (see, e.g., [Zaleznik, 2004]). In my career I have worked with both. What I learned from my experience can be summarized as follows:

- Leaders have their eyes on the future, managers on the present.
- Leaders drive change, managers maintain the *status quo*.
- Leaders focus on people, managers focus on policies and procedures.
- Leaders believe in continuous learning, managers rely on existing skills.
- Leaders inspire and motivate, managers give orders.
- Leaders encourage autonomy, managers request obedience.

> *"Management is doing things right;*
> *Leadership is doing the right things."*
> **Peter F. Drucker**, Management Consultant

Just to make things clear: I am not saying that managers are useless. Companies need managers as much as they need leaders. Focusing on the present, following existing processes, leveraging current skills are indeed important, and companies need people who make sure those tasks are diligently executed.

What scares me, though, are those managers who seem to switch off their brains when executing orders.

Some time ago I was discussing with a mid-level manager an order coming from his supervisor. The order sounded blatantly insane to me, and I believed it would have caused more harm than good to his employees if executed as it stood. I shared my concerns with the mid-level manager. His answer was: *"It doesn't matter what you or I think. It doesn't matter if it is right or wrong. It's an order, and I am expected to execute it."*

I still remember the goosebumps which suddenly developed on my skin. I remembered similar words being spoken in the past. Those words too referred to orders being executed without questioning them. It was at the Nuremberg Trial, in 1945.

✓ KEY TAKEAWAYS

1. Servant leaders focus on the growth of their people
2. Leading is different from managing
3. Orders can be questioned

THE SERVE MODEL

The core principles of Servant Leadership outlined in the previous chapter led me to develop and practice, over the years, a conceptual model—the **SERVE Model**—which is based on such principles.

This book presents and discusses the SERVE Model, summarizing why and how it contributed to developing high-performing teams and delivering extraordinary results.

In the five chapters that follow, we will explore the five pillars of the SERVE Model: **S**hare, **E**ncourage, **R**ecognize, **V**alue, and **E**mpathize.

Our review will focus on the use of the model in business environments. However, the SERVE Model can be easily generalized to other contexts, and later we will briefly consider its application to family members.

In the pages that follow I will often use the phrase *team leader*. That is because people whose role is to lead a team are the primary target group of the messages in this book. However, you do not need to formally lead a team to be a leader, and particularly a *servant* leader. Everyone can, and this book is about the how.

> *"A leader [...] is like a shepherd.*
> *He stays behind the flock, letting*
> *the most nimble go out ahead,*
> *whereupon the others follow, not*
> *realizing that all along they are*
> *being directed from behind."*
> **Nelson Mandela**, Political Leader

SHARE

When Somebody Shares, Everybody Wins

The letter **S** in the SERVE Model stands for **Share**. Sharing is an essential activity to overcome the limits of the individual and leverage the synergy of a team. None of us, regardless of how skilled, passionate and hard workers we are, can accomplish what an aligned, cooperative, and diverse team can.

> *"When somebody shares, everybody wins."*
>
> **Jim Rohn**, Entrepreneur & Motivational Speaker

There are at least 4 areas where sharing plays a pivotal role in forging the success of a team:

- Sharing Expectations

- Sharing Knowledge

- Sharing Information

- Sharing Results

In the following pages we will discuss each one of those areas in more details.

Share Expectations

The more unambiguously a leader shares with the team what he expects from them, the more likely it is the team will meet its targets without unnecessary (often expensive) misunderstandings.

> *"A goal properly set is halfway reached."*
>
> **Zig Ziglar**, Writer & Motivational Speaker

A couple of months ago, one of my direct reports told me her life would be much easier if all leaders were like me. A bit flattered by her remark, I asked her what she was alluding to. She said that when I share expectations with the team, everybody knows exactly what is expected, from whom, by when, and why.

Many organizations nowadays request employees to set individual SMART goals at the beginning of each fiscal year. The **SMART** acronym [Torrington *et al.*, 2014][2] stands for:

- **S**pecific
- **M**easurable
- **A**ppropriate
- **R**elevant
- **T**imebound

The core idea is to set goals that are well defined, clear and unambiguous (*specific*), whose progress towards accomplishment can be tracked in an objective way (*measurable*), are not impossible to achieve—even though they may require the employee to stretch—(*appropriate*), are important to the business (*relevant*), and have a clearly defined target date (*timebound*).

In addition to *individual* SMART goals, I find it helpful to set SMART goals also at team level.

- **Individual goals** make it clear to each team member what he is expected to accomplish in

---

[2] The 5 words that make up the SMART acronym vary by scholar and/or organization. For example, *Attainable*, *Actionable* or *Achievable* are often found instead of *Appropriate*; *Realistic* instead of *Relevant*; *Timely* or *Time-based* instead of *Timebound*. The core idea of SMART goals, however, does not change.

the following time period (typically the next 12 months).

- **Team goals** make it clear to all team members how their individual goals fit into the bigger picture and contribute to the success of the team.

It is responsibility of the team leader to ensure that individual and team goals are consistent and aligned, so that each individual goal met by a team member adds a valuable piece to the well-structured puzzle of a team goal.

In order to track progress of team goals throughout the year, I use a **Balanced Scorecard** [Kaplan and Norton, 1992], customized and tailored to the specific needs of the team.

The scorecard makes it possible to evaluate the performance of a team from 4 different perspectives:

- **Financial Perspective**: *how much value does the team create for the organization?*

- **Customer Perspective**: *how do customers see the team?*

- **Internal Business Perspective**: *how does the team support the business?*

- **Learning & Growth Perspective**: *how can the team continuously improve and expand the portfolio of services it offers?*

At the beginning of each fiscal year, I make sure that team goals are SMART, consistent and aligned with individual SMART goals, and trackable within the Balanced Scorecard framework.

Pushing for success in all four perspectives prevents sub-optimization, i.e. it avoids focusing only on some perspectives while neglecting the others. One of the lessons I learned in my career is that a team thrives when it is successful in *all* four perspectives, i.e. creates financial value for the organization, is appreciated by its customers, supports the business, and continuously improves and innovates to stay competitive on the market.

However, I also learned that a team should not become prisoner of its own goals. SMART goals, both at individual and team level, are certainly important, but should not be regarded as divine laws carved in stone. When extraordinary circumstances hit the team (e.g., a major economic crisis like the one we suffered in 2008, a pandemic like the one we experienced in 2020, or an unusually high turnover in the team), goals and scorecard should be adapted to the new situation and operations adjusted accordingly. The team leader is the one who can—and should—guarantee such flexibility.

Share Knowledge

I consider sharing knowledge as one of the vital activities for the growth of a team. In one of my last assignments, I encouraged knowledge sharing within the team and among its key stakeholders by means of 3 major schemes:

- Tag-Team Project Execution,
- Best Practice Meetings, and
- Community of Practice Sessions

"Sharing knowledge is the most fundamental act of friendship. Because it is a way you can give something without losing something."

Richard Stallman, Activist & Programmer

Tag-Team Project Execution refers to the way projects are assigned to team members. One of the major challenges a team leader faces is the need to ensure the same high-quality standards for all projects, regardless of who in the team works on them.

The dilemma here is whether to assign a new project to one of the most skilled (often most senior) members of the team (thus overloading her and depriving new members of the opportunity to build the necessary hands-on expertise), or to assign the project to a new member and run the risk of a sub-quality outcome due to her limited experience.

Our solution was to assign to each project a tag team made of a Primary Agent and a Secondary Agent. Since most of our projects dealt with modeling activities, the names we used were *Primary Modeler* and *Secondary Modeler*.

A new team member plays first the role of secondary modeler in a project where the primary modeler is one of the seniors. In this first phase the newbie observes the senior in action and learns from her the processes to be followed, the tools to be used, the way to interact with the customer, and all those activities—not necessarily merely technical—required when executing projects.

Once the new team member has built enough hands-on expertise, she gets assigned her first project as primary modeler. In this second phase the role of secondary modeler is played by one of the seniors, who acts as a coach for the newbie.

The tag-team approach is useful for making the onboarding process quicker and more efficient and ensures high-quality standards in project execution. Since any human being is subject to mistakes—even the most experienced and skilled ones—, the tag-team approach guarantees an extra pair of eyes to check data, assumptions, calculations, results, recommendations, etc. In other words, the tag-team approach minimizes the probability of errors, inaccuracies or omissions. This applies also when both primary and secondary modelers are experienced and skilled senior members of the team. For this reason, we utilized this approach in *all* our projects, and not only those involving new team members.

On a monthly basis, all members of the team used to get together for one of our **Best Practice Meetings**.

The agenda of those meetings was pretty much open: any one of us could share with the others any new tools, algorithms, topics, and/or lessons learned in the previous month. Anything we thought the others could benefit from. Over the years, we shared high-level overviews of software packages the team could take advantage of, papers or books worth reading, videos worth watching, training classes worth taking, errors made and how they were fixed, issues faced and how they were overcome.

We stored what was shared during Best Practice Meetings into a shared folder to make contents accessible to those who could not attend the meeting live as well as to future team members who could benefit from the best practices.

Best Practice Meetings ensured that the most important lessons learned by a single member of the team were shared with the others, thus nurturing a continuous growth for the team in its entirety.

While participation to Best Practice Meetings was generally limited to team members, our **Community of Practice (CoP) Sessions** targeted a much larger audience.

CoPs aim at gathering together people who share common interests, for example software (e.g., SharePoint, Tableau), technology fields (e.g., discrete-event simulation, computer vision), areas of expertise (e.g., assembly, paint), etc.

As a consequence, the very first step when creating a new CoP is to define what such common interest (or interests) is, and who are the people who should, or would like to, be part of it.

Our CoP Sessions did not have only the objective of sharing knowledge with key stakeholders. They had also a marketing purpose: make current and potential customers aware of the services the team has been, is and will be offering in the near future. We will talk about this aspect in more details in the next pages when discussing how to share results.

The second step we took with our CoP was to select the topics to be discussed in our monthly sessions in order to create an agenda for the entire year. Since our sessions had also a marketing purpose, we gave participants the opportunity to select the topics they wanted to see discussed. This was done by means of a survey we ran a few weeks before the start of a new fiscal year. Our CoP Sessions were structured as monthly events, so we had to select 12 topics for the new year. When needed, topics requested by our customers were complemented with additional topics selected by our team.

Once finalized, the list of topics—with associated dates, times and presenters—was shared with all CoP members. CoP Sessions were recorded and videos shared later with all CoP members[3]. This allowed

---

[3] Obviously, video recording took place after ensuring full compliance with privacy rules.

people who missed a session to watch it at their own convenience, and people who attended it live to access it again, if desired.

As in the case of SMART goals, I find it vitally important for the team not to become constrained by its own processes, policies and procedures. If circumstances demand special topics to be discussed in a CoP Session, I recommend the team to be open and willing to adjust its CoP Agenda accordingly.

This was the case in 2020, when the COVID-19 pandemic demanded us to rearrange our CoP Agenda and set up a special CoP Session on how to use discrete-event simulation to analyze social distancing violations on assembly lines.

Share Information

According to the Cambridge dictionary, *information* is defined as *"facts about a situation, person, event, etc."*.

This definition fits perfectly the point I would like to make here: very few things have the power to destroy a well-functioning team as **rumors** do. That is why I find it extremely important to share *facts*—the *truth*—to promptly combat rumors, gossip, and fake news.

I am definitely not saying you should disclose confidential information, intellectual property, or privacy-protected data. Not at all. Each and every team member *must* diligently and unconditionally adhere to compliance regulations.

> *"Fire and swords are slow engines of destruction, compared to the tongue of a Gossip."*
> **Richard Steele**, Dramatist

What I am talking about here is for the team leader to ensure that factual and objective information is shared to prevent the spreading of rumors which have the potential to undermine the well-functioning of the team.

Some time ago, an international company went through a major internal reorganization. Information about the scope of the reorganization and its impact on individual jobs and responsibilities was poorly communicated by upper management and human resources. Rumors, gossip, fake information started to spread like an avalanche. All of a sudden, everybody's job seemed to be at risk. In the chaos that followed, many employees, uncertain about their future and worried for their families, started looking for job opportunities on the external market. Top performers, the ones with the best skills and most expertise, did not struggle much to find a rewarding job in another company, in many cases ending up working for direct competitors. Deprived of its best talents, the international company could do nothing but replace their vacant positions with less experienced and less skilled employees, with obvious negative consequences on daily operations. Better information could have limited the disaster.

I made a similar error years ago. One of the best performers in our team was long due for a promotion. I knew he wanted it badly, and he fully deserved it. He had done an extraordinary job while in our team. However, receiving all formal approvals for a promotion may take a long time, especially in large companies like the one we worked for. In that case, it took *too* long. Before I could surprise him with the good news of his promotion, he surprised me with the bad (at least for me) news of his resignation. Frustrated with a promotion that seemed not to arrive, he had applied to another company, and got selected. Four weeks later he was gone, and it was also my fault. I failed to inform him about all the work we were doing behind the scenes to give him the promotion he deserved.

For me, this was a lesson learned. Since then, I have been very open and transparent with the team, especially when it comes to job changes, budget proposals, and strategic plans. Transparent and open information sharing leads to trust and builds camaraderie: we are all playing on the same side, and everybody in the team knows that.

Sharing information does not apply only to relatively infrequent events like job changes, budget proposals or strategic plans. Sharing information is useful also when it comes to daily tasks executed by the team.

Following the **Agile Methodology**, one of my reports gets full credit for initiating, a few years ago, **Daily Stand-Up Meetings** [Beedle, 1997] in our team. During such short meetings (typically lasting 15 to 20 minutes, same place and same time every day), each team member informs the others on what he has accomplished in the past 24 hours, what he plans to accomplish in the next 24 hours, and which issues he is currently facing.

Daily stand-up meetings are useful to quickly share relevant information, check opportunities for collaboration, leverage synergies whenever possible, and combat rumors. However, it must be said that daily stand-up meetings may become ineffective or last too long when a team is made of 10 or more members [geekbot, 2020].

Share Results

If nobody knows what a team accomplished, it is like success did not happen. That is why I recommend investing the necessary time and energy in sharing team results with management, peers, and customers. Sharing results does not only fulfill the goal of informing key stakeholders of what the team did. It has at least two additional purposes:

- First, it is a powerful marketing vehicle. When potential customers are informed of what the team accomplished, it is likely they will request their services in the near future.

- Second, sharing success is an opportunity to recognize team members for their accomplishments. We will talk later about the importance of Recognition, the letter **R** in the SERVE model.

With those purposes in mind, a couple of years ago our team created a comprehensive **communication strategy** to ensure that all relevant stakeholders were kept regularly informed of what the team was doing. Our communication strategy was made of 4 main components:

- A **Project Tracking Site**, with an up-to-date list of all projects the team was working on, and their progress status. We implemented workflows to send automatic emails to relevant parties (e.g., competency leads) whenever a new project was started or an existing one completed.

- A monthly electronic **Newsletter**, which informed all interested parties of projects executed, training classes offered, development activities in progress, new videos released, and any other significant team accomplishment. We made sure that the newsletter distribution list was always up to date to reflect organizational changes and job replacements.

- A **Team Page** on the company-internal social networking tool, with posted content similar to that of our newsletter, but without the constraint of only one delivery per month. A social networking tool, compared to a newsletter, offers also the advantage of allowing readers to interact with a post by means of likes and comments.

- **Success Story Videos**, with our customers talking about how our team helped them solve their problems and generate benefits for their unit. Success Story Videos, short in duration (they rarely exceeded 3 minutes) and crisp in their message, proved to be an extraordinarily powerful marketing instrument. A customer telling others how great a team is has a much larger impact than the same words said by the team leader or by any team member.

> *"Communication is your ticket to success, if you pay attention and learn to do it effectively."*
> **Theo Gold**, Writer & Motivational Speaker

The 4 main components listed above (*Project Tracking Site*, *Newsletter*, *Team Page*, and *Success Story Videos*) were complemented by the CoP Sessions we mentioned earlier, training classes (both virtual and classroom), presentations by team members at major events (both external and internal to the organization), etc.

A comprehensive, relentless and targeted communication strategy is one of the main reasons why we succeeded, in a time span of only five years, in quadrupling the number of annual projects we deployed.

✓ KEY TAKEAWAYS

1. Set SMART goals (both individual & team)
2. Encourage tag-team project execution
3. Ensure sharing of best practices
4. Select participants and topics of CoP Sessions
5. Guarantee flexibility (SMART goals, CoP Agenda)
6. Combat rumors with fact-based information
7. Schedule daily stand-up team meetings if team size fits
8. Create & apply a comprehensive Communication Strategy

ENCOURAGE

Lifelong Learning

The first of the two letters **E** in the SERVE Model stands for **Encourage**. More precisely, it stands for **Encourage to Learn**.

In October 2016 I started my Executive Master of Business Administration (EMBA) at Frankfurt School of Finance & Management. More than 18 years had elapsed since the day I completed my Master's in Engineering. More than 14 since I received my Doctorate Degree. In October 2016 I was 43 years old.

I remember the look of astonishment many friends gave me at the time. *"Are you really going to pursue a second Master's Degree?"*, *"You have already a PhD, why do you need an EMBA?"*, *"Don't you think you are a bit old to go back to school?"*. An endless sequence of questions like these.

No. I do not think there is an age when a person is too old to learn something. One of my cousins, Meyra, received her second Master's Degree in Philosophy when she was 85, and I am deeply proud of her.

I believe that a day, any day, is wasted if we do not learn something or someone new, be it a new piece of information, a new skill, a new person, a new experience.

> *"Live as if you were to die tomorrow.*
> *Learn as if you were to live forever."*
> **Mahatma Gandhi**, Politician & Philosopher

I have always been a strong advocate of **lifelong learning**[4], and one of the reasons why back in 2016 I chose the Frankfurt School EMBA Program was the lifelong learning opportunity the Program offers: after completing their EMBA, Frankfurt School Alumni are given the opportunity to take one course per year for free. Needless to say, I already took advantage of such opportunity and attended their course on *Digital Transformation* in 2019.

The Greek philosopher Heraclitus once said that *"change is the only constant in life"*. This is particularly true in today's world, where much of what will happen in the next few decades is inevitable, driven

---

[4] See e.g. my short video on YouTube: www.youtube.com/watch?v= DbZEp1jVJZw&feature=youtu.be.

by technological trends already in motion [Kelly, 2016].

Leaders must understand that change is inevitable, and must prepare for it [Kotter, 2012]. I am fully convinced that the only way to be prepared for change is to keep learning, relentlessly and passionately.

The Learning Culture

To face continuous change and thrive in a market which keeps evolving at an ever-increasing speed, it is usually not enough to have only one or two team members exploring new fields, learning new skills, or practicing with new software. What is needed is a **learning culture** to be embraced by the entire team. And the team leader is the one who should take the responsibility to develop such culture and lead by example.

Inspired by Google's **"20% Time"** policy[5] [Rahrovani et al., 2018], which encouraged Google engineers to spend 20% of their paid work time on personal projects (major products like Gmail and

---

[5] Google's "20% Time" policy was discontinued in 2013. A similar concept was pioneered by 3M back in 1948. The time 3M required its employees to dedicate to a personal interest was 15%.

Google News are the outcome of such personal projects), our team members were asked to dedicate a few working hours every week to explore new software, techniques and algorithms of their choice, which had the potential to expand the portfolio of services offered by the team, and ultimately increase our business.

> *"The mind that opens to a new idea never returns to its original size."*
> **Albert Einstein**, Physicist

According to the **70:20:10 Model** [Arets *et al.*, 2016], workplace learning is made of:

- **Experiential Learning** (70%): employees are learning and practicing while doing the job.
- **Social Learning** (20%): employees learn with and through others, by taking advantage of cooperation, mentoring and coaching.
- **Formal Learning** (10%): employees learn through formal training courses.

The ratios are not set in stone and vary heavily by organizations, with reported ratios of 40-30-30, 50-30-20, 60-20-20, etc. [DeakinCo., 2018].

I personally believe that the ratios depend greatly on the type of work the team is—or will be—doing.

When team members are investigating a new technology or a new software, opportunities for effective social learning may be very limited within the organization, simply because there are no experts yet in that technology or that software.

Also, if the risks associated to an error on the job are very high (as is the case, for example, of commercial airplane pilots), the ratio of formal learning may exceed that of on-the job practicing, at least during the first months or years in the job.

Irrespective of their relative ratios, the team learning scheme our team developed years ago took advantage of all three components of the *70-20-10 Model*:

- **Experiential Learning**: in addition to *Tag-Team Project Execution* (see the Share Knowledge section above), we created a network of *Subject Matter Experts* (SMEs) from Universities and Research Institutes. Our approach consisted in signing collaboration contracts with those experts for a fixed amount of consultancy hours per year. When facing major challenges or exploring new fields in their job, team members had the possibility to consult with one of the SMEs for guidance, advice, or simply to share ideas, discuss alternatives, or receive feedback. Collaboration with SMEs proves very effective especially when team members explore areas where no experts exist in the organization.

- **Social Learning**: in addition *to Best Practice Meetings* and *Community of Practice Sessions* (see the Share Knowledge section above), which encourage cross-pollination within the team (and beyond it), we took advantage of three other opportunities:

    o *Conferences, Symposia, Fora*: participating in such events gives team members the opportunity to meet other practitioners, exchange ideas with them, and learn from their experiences (their successes and—even more relevant—their **failures**). I personally took the initiative to create and distribute one-pagers summarizing the main takeaways from an event, with hyperlinks to the most relevant presentations or videos, and the names and emails of the most useful contacts made at the event.

o *Consortia*: participating in EU-funded projects as well as in consortia at global, continental, national, or regional level enables collaboration with other organizations, sometimes even with competitors. This offers insights into how other industries function and other organizations operate, their strategies and their best practices, and nurtures innovative, **out-of-the-box thinking**. Being part of a diverse group was one of the most valuable experiences I made during my EMBA days. Our class at Frankfurt School was made of professionals from 17 different nationalities and a large variety of very diverse industries and fields: from banking to consultancy firms, from pharmaceutical companies to automotive manufacturers. This kind of experience encourages trying new things and explore new paths, thus silencing those few words each one of us has heard at least once in our lives and that kill any entrepreneurship spirit: "*We have done things always this way here*".

- o *Mentoring & Coaching*: large organizations often offer internal mentoring and/or coaching opportunities for their employees. I personally use to mentor four or five people per year in addition to students. Mentors and coaches provide different perspectives and diverse points of view, which are extremely important when multiple perspectives need to be taken into account.

- **Formal Learning**: in addition to books and journals shared by team members or purchased by the team, and formal courses, virtual and classroom, offered within the organization, we took advantage of the large and relatively inexpensive offer of Massive Open Online Courses, or **MOOCs**. Nowadays, there is a vast market of affordable remote learning opportunities on a variety of topics and at a variety of educational levels on platforms like Coursera, edX, Udacity, DataCamp, or Udemy, just to name a few. Formal learning gave team members the foundational know-how to be complemented with hands-on practical experience built on projects.

A well-balanced mix of experiential, social and formal learning made it possible for our team to expand our services from exclusively discrete-event simulation modeling to new fields like data analytics, virtual reality, geographic information systems, and machine learning. Team members grew their skills and expertise and became benchmarking examples to other teams.

✓ **KEY TAKEAWAYS**

1. Be a role model of lifelong learning
2. Promote Experiential-Social-Formal learning in the team
3. Establish a network of SMEs to act as go-to consultants
4. Share takeaways from events through one-pagers
5. Learn from successes, learn even more from failures
6. Encourage collaboration with diverse partners
7. Take advantage of existing MOOCs

RECOGNIZE

The Power of a Thank You

The letter **R** in the SERVE Model stands for **Recognition**.

Recognition does not necessarily mean red carpets, big stages, large clapping audiences, and shiny recognition trophies. Sometimes two words as simple as *THANK YOU* can make the difference in the ears of those hearing them.

> *"Appreciation can change a day, even change a life. Your willingness to put it into words is all that is necessary."*
> **Margaret Cousins**, Editor, Journalist & Writer

A couple of years ago, a major company started an initiative to encourage employees to take the time and thank their fellow workers. **Thank-You cards** were made available for free to any employees requesting them.

The idea, simple and relatively inexpensive, gave every single employee in the company the opportunity to recognize others and be recognized. It also sent a clear message on the importance upper management gave to employee recognition.

The same company also implemented in its intranet a system that enables employees to give **virtual badges** to their coworkers. Different badge types allow employees to be thanked for a work well done, welcomed to a new team, congratulated for a major accomplishment, recognized for their team-player attitude, celebrated for having gone the extra mile in a specific activity, and so on.

What I find relevant (and rewarding for the employee receiving the badge) is that virtual badges are permanently displayed on the employee profile in the company's internal system. Unlike Thank-You cards, which are a private communication between sender and receiver (even though I saw employees displaying in their offices or at their desks the cards they received), virtual badges are visible to all employees, and make therefore the recognition a more public and potentially more rewarding event for those receiving the badges.

Cultural Differences

I have been living in Germany since 2007 and became also a German citizen back in 2016. Having lived in three different countries (Italy, United States and Germany) and having worked with people from very diverse cultural backgrounds, I have to admit that recognizing employees is not one of the strengths of most German managers, writing it in a polite way.

I typically do not like generalizations, which are often the consequence of stereotypes and sometimes the offspring of racism. Nonetheless, the joke about German bosses expressing their appreciation when not complaining about their employees (*"nicht geschimpft ist auch genug gelobt"*, which roughly translates into *"not telling people off is adequate praise"*) is often not far from the truth. One of the reasons why I mention such joke in this book is that I hope that German managers, when reading about it, will contribute to changing the stereotype with their actions.

If Germany sits on the lower end of an imaginary Recognition Scale, countries like India sit next to its top. I have worked very closely with Indian colleagues in the past 15 years, and what I noticed is that recognition is so common in India that those who stand out are not those who get recognized, but rather those who do *not*.

Let's take as an example the virtual badges I talked about in the previous section. If the average German employee displays 2 or 3 such badges on her profile, the average employee in India typically displays 20 or 30 of them. The average employee in the United States usually stands somewhere in the middle.

I am not saying that one approach is wrong and the other is right, even though I personally believe that Germans should recognize more and Indians less. The point I would like to make here, though, is that there are significant **cultural differences** when it comes to recognition, and leaders of multi-cultural teams need to be aware of them.

> *"Experiencing different cultures is one of the best things a human being can do. It puts your whole world into perspective."*
> **Stephanie Gilmore**, Professional Surfer

An employee from Latin America would most likely be happy to be publicly recognized by a large audience with a long round of applause. The same scenario may create significant embarrassment in an employee from Scandinavia.

Money is not the Main Driver

There are many ways to recognize people in addition to handing over Thank-You cards or sending virtual badges.

One obvious form of recognition for an employee is a promotion, salary increase, or extra payment triggered by Payment-By-Results (PBR) schemes or Performance-Related Plans (PRP) [Torrington *et al.*, 2014].

> *"Cash matters in people's lives, but it's not all that matters. What really matters in the workplace is helping employees feel appreciated."*
>
> **Amy Whillans**, Harvard Business School Researcher

However, financial incentives are rarely the main motivator [Kohn, 1993]. Most people rather prefer jobs where they feel appreciated, have the opportunity to develop new skills, or see that they are contributing to a higher purpose. When I joined John

Deere back in 2002, for example, the main driver for me was not the yearly salary I was offered (even though, I confess, it was *one* of the drivers). It was the opportunity to contribute towards fighting global hunger by helping build agricultural machines to seed, grow and harvest food.

Here below I am listing some of the recognition practices I came across or personally used in my professional career:

- **Anniversary Gifts** or **Gift Cards** are used to celebrate work anniversaries (typically multiples of 5 or 10 years). Employees select a gift from a given catalogue or a gift card from a list of popular stores or restaurant chains. The value of the gift or the amount on the card usually increase with the number of years in the company. This recognition practice, very popular in the United States, has the disadvantage of being based exclusively on seniority, unrelated to individual performance or merit. Also, when it comes to gift cards, this practice does not differ much from a one-time extra payment, but without the flexibility offered by cash (the amount on the card must be spent in a specific store or restaurant chain and, often, before a given expiry date).

- **Reserved Parking Spots**. This practice is popular in the United States and, in general, wherever a large portion of employees drive to work. One or more parking spots, typically those located most closely to the workplace entrance (and therefore most coveted by commuters), are reserved to the "employee(s) of the month" (the time period may vary, I have seen spots reserved to the "employee of the year" as well as to the "employee of the quarter"). This recognition practice has at least 2 advantages: 1) it rewards performance, not seniority, and 2) it is visible to everybody entering the building, thus publicly honoring the recognized employee and motivating other employees to accomplish the same.

- **Honorary Titles** typically do not bring any tangible benefits (no gift cards or reserved parking spots) to the ones who receive them. Nonetheless, I personally find them an excellent way to give the stage to high performers, increase motivation among employees, and foster emulation. To this recognition practice belong titles like "Employee of the Month", "Manager of the Quarter", "Salesman of the Year", and so on, in different combinations of titles and time periods. Honorary titles are often assigned during large venues where recognized employees are usually handed over a celebrative medal, plaque or trophy in front of a large clapping audience. Like reserved parking spots, this recognition practice rewards performance and is highly visible to other employees. On top of that, honorary titles are nice awards to mention in a resume.

- **Certificates of Accomplishment.** This recognition practice is generally associated to the completion of a training class or a hands-on project work. In one of my past assignments, we created a set of training classes which required trainees to watch a series of videos, take a multiple-choice test, and practice with a hands-on assignment. Successful completion of all required steps led to the trainee receiving a printed certificate. Over the years, when visiting company locations all around the world, I was pleased to see employees proudly displaying in their offices or at their desks the certificates we handed over to them.

Several other recognition practices exist, but the goal of this chapter is not to provide an exhaustive list of all possible ways to recognize employees. The goal here is rather to motivate and inspire leaders to recognize their team members and reward their accomplishments.

Team Recognition

Recognition practices like the ones mentioned in the previous section are typically organized and managed at corporate or division level.

In addition to them, I find it extremely important to have sound recognition practices also at team level. Team-level recognition, compared to corporate- or division-level celebrations, is more intimate and allows employees to be appreciated and recognized by their direct manager or manager's manager in presence of their fellow team members and/or families.

> *"An employee's motivation is a direct result of the sum of interactions with his or her manager."*
>
> **Bob Nelson**, Writer & Motivational Speaker

In my entire career as a manager, I never missed to organize at least one Team Recognition Event per year. Even during the COVID-19 pandemic, in 2020, we had our team event, even though in a virtual form.

When dealing with team-level events, I recommend team leaders to pay special attention to a couple of things:

1. Make sure you know how to pronounce correctly the name of the people you will be recognizing. As hilarious as it may sound, with large, international teams, a team leader may not know how to pronounce a name, especially when most interactions among team members take place via email and the person to be recognized is a recent addition to the team. In my opinion, there are very few things worse than publicly mispronouncing someone's name, especially when recognizing this person. A couple of examples I was the earwitness of: first, a German employee by the name of *Jürgen* (a popular masculine name in Germany where *Jür* is pronounced approximately like *your* and *ge* as in *Gary*) was publicly called *jargon*. Second, an Indian coworker named *Sachin* (*sach* to be pronounced as in *such*) was addressed as *suck-in*. In both cases the mispronounced name led to embarrassment (for most team members immediately; for the team leader later, when the

mistake was reported to him), and to a bitter feeling of disenchantment for the recognized employee who felt as if the leader did not even know him.

2. Tailor your speech to the employee you are recognizing. The large majority of the recognition events I attended ended up with some high-level manager on a brightly illuminated stage cheering an employee with a vigorous handshake and words like *"Thank you so much!"*, *"We are grateful for the great job you made!"*, *"We are impressed by the exceptional results you achieved"*. In general, an endless, decontextualized sequence of *fantastic, terrific, magnificent, superb, excellent, extraordinary, outstanding, supreme, wonderful, marvelous, gorgeous*, etc. I find this behavior quite irritating. More than once I was tempted to raise my hand and ask the manager to spend a few words to better explain to the audience *why* the employee was being recognized. The reason why I eventually never asked the question is that I was damn sure the manager had absolutely no clue about what the employee actually did. Maybe he did not even know the name of the employee until a few minutes earlier. Acting like this can

undermine the core purpose of the recognition event, that is to celebrate an employee for something he did extraordinarily well. Before going on stage and recognizing someone, I spend the necessary time to learn what this person did to deserve the recognition. If the recognition is for a project, what was the objective of the project, what was its outcome, how does that project fit in the company's strategy, who else worked on it? If the recognition is for some collaboration activity, what was the goal of the collaboration, who did the employee collaborate with, what made him stand out, what did the collaboration lead to? I could give you many more examples, but I believe you got the point. For some people such recognitions are key moments in their professional lives, moments they will possibly remember for many years to come, maybe forever. What they expect to hear is their name (correctly pronounced!) and a few words of praise for what they did. A handshake and an anonymous "thank you" will probably leave a feeling of disillusion and bitterness, no matter how shiny the recognition trophy is.

✓ KEY TAKEAWAYS

1. Take the time to say Thank You
2. Be aware of cultural differences
3. Financial incentives are rarely the main motivator
4. Reward Your Team
5. Make sure you know how to pronounce names
6. Tailor your words to the person you recognize

VALUE

Everyone is a Winner

The letter **V** in the SERVE Model stands for **Value**. More precisely, it stands for **Value your Employees**.

Valuing employees means leveraging their strengths, their unique skills, the activities they excel at. Finding the right role for each member to play in a team is, from my perspective, one of the vital few activities of a leader. This is evident in sports like football, where each one of the 11 players has a well-defined role, different from the roles of the other 10 players. The goalkeeper most likely will not perform equally well when playing as a striker, and a center-midfielder probably will not be playing at his best as a wing-back defender.

Valuing employees for their unique capabilities comes easier if we realize that each and every one of us, without exception, is indeed a winner.

Several years ago, during a 7-course Christmas lunch in Rome, Gabriele—the father of one of my best friends—said something I will never forget: *Everyone is a winner, all of us.*

I must admit that this statement did not make much sense to me when I first heard it. My mind rumbled instantly to refugees, clochards, orphans. Can a refugee who lost everything be considered a winner? Is a homeless clochard a winner? A kid who grew up in an orphanage without parents, is he a winner?

Yes, yes and yes, answered Gabriele. I must have stared at him with the same skeptic look of someone who just got paid with 15-Euro bills[6]. He smiled and explained me his point.

> *"Everybody is a genius. But if you judge a fish by its ability to climb a tree, it will live its whole life believing that it is stupid."*
> **Albert Einstein**, Physicist

In the process of human fertilization, 300 to 500 million spermatozoa race to the ovum, but one—only one, emphasized Gabriele while raising his right index

---

[6] In case you are not familiar with Euro banknotes, 15-Euro bills do not exist.

finger—penetrates the ovum. Each one of us is the final product of the spermatozoon that won the race. All of us are gold-medal winners in a race with half a billion participants. The refugee, the clochard, the orphan are indeed winners.

Gabriele was absolutely right.

Several years ago, I had a hard time with one of my team's members. A top performer himself, this guy wanted to team up only with other top performers. He used to make derogatory remarks on other team members, tagging them as *incompetent*, *inept*, *unable*, *detrimental to the project*. His attitude (and words) quickly led to friction and discontent in the team, which came to an end only when the guy was moved to another team. He was unable to detect the unique skills the ones he tagged as incompetent indeed had.

The point I would like to make here is that too often leaders focus only on **top performers**, the ones whose skills are blatantly above the average. It is much harder and time consuming to spot the unique talents of all other team members. Because each one of us has unique skills, each one of us is, indeed, a winner.

One Team, Many Roles

Identifying which activities each team member is best at requires patience, close observation, and willingness to accept the risks of wrong assignments.

In my career, I have been leading several teams and been the member of many more. I have observed at least 7 distinct roles in action.

- **The Movie Star**. The Movie Star thrives when she is on stage, standing in the spotlight in front of large audiences. Humility is usually not one of her strengths, but this does not necessarily mean that the Movie Star is arrogant. The Movie Star simply needs attention, praise, recognition. Her being at ease in front of large audiences, often combined with above-standard presentation skills, make the Movie Star the ideal candidate for running recognition events, presenting at conferences, reporting team accomplishments together with— or instead of—the team leader. We will talk about the importance of Delegation in the next section.

- **The Professor.** The Professor loves teaching his peers, sharing knowledge, and learning new skills. He is enthused by knowledge-sharing activities like *Best Practice Meetings* and *Community of Practice Sessions* (see section on Share

Knowledge), and takes often the lead in organizing and carrying out experiential, social and formal learning initiatives (see section on The Learning Culture). The Professor is a linchpin in creating the necessary momentum to turn individual growth into team growth, especially when he is paired with a new team member in *Tag-Team Project Execution* (see section on Share Knowledge).

- **The Caregiver.** The Caregiver is the one the team can always count on in case of problems like tight deadlines, unexpected absence of team members (e.g., due to sickness), a sudden workload increase, etc. The Caregiver is the first one to raise her hand when help is needed and work must be redistributed. The Caregiver does not generally enjoy the spotlight, and is usually not driven by the opportunity to teach others or learn new skills. What drives her is the desire to help others and feel useful. The Caregiver plays a vital role for the team when deadlines have to be met despite unexpected, unfavorable circumstances.

- **The Number-Cruncher.** The Number-Cruncher feeds on numbers. Software packages like Excel, Tableau, PowerBI, Statistica, and programming languages like Python, R, Java are his food. In today's world, where Big Data and Machine Learning are spreading everywhere and *"the most interesting emerging religion is Dataism"* [Harari, 2017], Number-Crunchers are in high demand in nearly every single organization and industry. Excellent programmers and modelers, Number-Crunchers usually do not feel comfortable in the spotlight and often prefer working alone, but they are vital for the success of the team. It is responsibility of the team leader to ensure that Number-Crunchers do not work in isolation, but rather share their knowledge and expertise with the rest of the team.

- **The Customer-Focused.** The Customer-Focused would do everything to please her customers and make them happy. She typically adapts her working hours to be in synch with the customer (especially when the customer is in a different time zone). The product or service being delivered (a physical item, a model, a report, etc.) is tailored to the desires of the customer. The Customer-Focused is critical in ensuring that customers return to the team for new products and/or services. However, it is responsibility of the team leader to make sure that delighting customers does not turn into unprofitable operations for the team. In other words, the team leader needs to ensure that focus on customers and focus on profit are properly balanced.

- **The Social Buddy.** The Social Buddy is the one who can potentially turn a group of coworkers into a group of friends. He is the one organizing team lunches and dinners, celebrating birthdays and anniversaries, and proposing team-building activities (we will talk about team-building activities in more details in the next chapter). The coffee machine (if there is one) is the center of gravity of the Social Buddy, and most of his social interactions take place while holding a steaming cup of coffee in his hand. The Social Buddy focuses most of his energies on strengthening relationships and building his network. The team leader must ensure that social interactions do not turn into fertile ground for rumors and gossip. Also, the team leader should leverage the network of the Social Buddy as an opportunity to expand the team's customer base.

- **The Innovator.** The Innovator is naturally attracted by novelties: new technologies, products, discoveries, inventions. She is usually a technology enthusiast, and aspires to own the most recent version of any popular product, be it an automobile, a smartphone, a TV. Her desire to try and use novelties can be a stimulus for the entire team to explore new fields, tools, techniques, and eventually expand the portfolio of products and/or services the team can offer to its customers. It is responsibility of the team leader to leverage the enthusiasm of the Innovator and direct it towards activities potentially profitable for the team.

> *"The strength of the team is each individual member. The strength of each member is the team."*
>
> **Phil Jackson**, Professional Basketball Executive

The 7 roles outlined above are not disjoint boxes with each team member falling into one, and only one, of them. I have seen Innovators who are excellent Number-Crunchers, and Social Buddies who are outstanding Movie Stars, just to mention a couple of examples. The 7 roles are not meant to be used to pigeonholing people and attaching them a permanent tag. The point I would like to make here is that knowing the core role (or mix of roles) of each one of the team members can help the leader in leveraging their distinct characteristics to the benefit of the entire team.

The 7 roles listed above are mainly related to personalities and innate emotional patterns [Goleman, 1995], they are not necessarily connected to specific skills. Some people possess by birth analytical minds (Number-Crunchers), others connect well with people and are easy to make friends with (Social Buddies), others are naturally inclined to help others (Caregivers).

Personalities are more difficult (but not impossible) to change, new skills can be learned all life long (see section on Lifelong Learning).

Team leaders should be aware of the core role(s) their team members can best play, and then leverage both their personalities and skills to the benefit of the entire team. Leveraging strengths does not mean ignoring weaknesses, and lifelong learning should focus on growing strengths as well as on closing gaps, wherever relevant ones are found.

Delegation

Valuing employees means also trusting them, and trust eventually leads to delegation. Managers who do not delegate responsibilities to their team become a danger to the company, to the team, and even to themselves. Let's see why.

- **Danger to the company.** No delegation easily leads to micro-management, that is managers doing tasks meant to be handled by their team. A micro-manager can quickly turn into the main bottleneck for the team [Maniccia, 1993], and the team into a bottleneck for all those departments and units in the company which depend on the team's output. Unmet deadlines and hasty execution can put the entire company in danger, especially when the micro-managed team plays a crucial role in the company's operations.

- **Danger to the team.** A micro-manager working on the tasks of his team deprives team members of the opportunity to practice and learn, and eventually develop skills and expertise which are essential for the team to grow and prosper in the long term (see section on Lifelong Learning).

- **Danger to themselves.** Micro-managers are likely to become indispensable and hard to promote, sometimes simply because they have not trained anybody in the team to be their successors.

In his book *The One-Minute Manager Meets the Monkey* [Blanchard *et al.*, 1990], Ken Blanchard compares tasks to be executed to **monkeys** hanging on someone's back. The more managers get rid of their people's monkeys through delegation, the more time they will have for their work and their people, the more successful they and their team will eventually be.

> *"The best way to develop responsibility in people is to give them responsibility."*
> **Ken Blanchard**, Author & Motivational Speaker

Psychological Safety

Valuing people means accepting their **failures** when they happen.

As written in the INTRODUCTION, failures are not necessarily negative if people (and teams) learn and grow through them. In 2019, while attending an innovation event in Copenhagen, I had the opportunity to visit what they call the *Museum of Failure* (museumoffailure.com), a collection of failed products and services from around the world.

Innovation and progress require risks to be taken and failures to be accepted. What is important is for the leader to create a culture of **psychological safety** in the team, to build the necessary conditions for employees to be willing to say what is on their minds, take risks, and accept failures without fear of punishment or finger-pointing.

> *"Psychological safety is a belief that one will not be punished or humiliated for speaking up with ideas, questions, concerns or mistakes."*
> **Amy Edmondson**, Harvard Professor

The phrase *psychological safety* was coined by Harvard Business School Professor Amy Edmondson [Edmondson, 1999]. A psychologically safe workplace is not merely a place where employees are free from discrimination and harassment (which is a necessary prerequisite). It is a place where employees are free to speak up and express their own ideas for improvement.

Respect

Valuing people means also respecting them. *All* of them.

Years ago, I had the opportunity to take part in a hands-on assembly training. For one week, engineers, managers and shopfloor workers would team up and build on their own, as a team of seven, one of the factory products. Actually, we were not left completely on our own, since an experienced instructor was always with us to make sure our product would meet the same high-quality standards of all other products built in the plant. While practicing as assemblers, all of us were wearing work suites, the same suites worn every day by any shopfloor worker in that facility.

One day, *The Magnificent Seven* (as we jokingly called ourselves those days) went together for lunch. On the way to the cafeteria we ran into one of the factory managers, a guy I had known for several years. I cheerfully greeted him as I was used to, and called him by his first name. To my surprise, the guy had a fleeting glance at us and continued on his way without returning the greetings. I was puzzled.

A few days later, once the training was over, I ran into the same guy again in the cafeteria. This time, I was wearing my standard business suit, as most managers do. This time, the guy returned my greetings with a friendly smile on his face. I approached him and gently asked what happened a few days earlier, when we crossed paths in the factory yard. His answer was: *"I am sorry, I didn't recognize you. I thought it was just a group of assemblers"*.

Let me write it one more time. Please read the sentence aloud, spelling it out. *I thought it was just a group of assemblers.*

I was more disturbed by his words when he tried to justify himself than by his manners when he missed to return my greetings.

> *"Treat people the way you want to be treated. Talk to people the way you want to be talked to. Respect is earned, not given."*
>
> **Jenny Garrett**, Career Coach & Leadership Trainer

Unfortunately, such a behavior is not uncommon in some managers. Over the years, I have observed disrespect expressed in many different ways, shapes and forms: employees waiting half an hour in front of their boss' closed door, with the boss blatantly ignoring appointment times; managers not returning emails or phone calls from lower-grade employees; supervisors intimidating their employees by yelling at them.

No team can be successful when there is no full respect between the leader and her team members as well as respect among team members.

One of my former supervisors taught me an important lesson years ago. When going to the factory floor for one of his *Gemba*[7] *Walks* [Womack, 2011], he

---

[7] *Gemba* (or *genba*) in Japanese means *the actual place*. In **Lean Manufacturing**, *Gemba Walks* refer to the action of going to the

used to greet workers one by one, friendly shaking their hands, introducing himself by his first name, and thanking each one of them for the value they were generating to the company.

Both Italy (where I come from) and Germany (where I have been living for the past 13 years) are highly hierarchical societies. Coworkers typically call each other by their last names (usually preceded by their academic titles) and use the courtesy form when talking. You can imagine how untypical this guy sounded to me whenever I heard him approaching workers with words like: "*Hi, I am Tom. Thank you so much for all the work you do every day to make this company even greater. What's your name?*".

What I recommend to each one of you is to treat all the people you interact with, both at work and privately, as if they were your CEO. Have a word with shopfloor workers, cleaning staff, security guards, cafeteria personnel, mailmen. Show them, every day, respect and appreciation for the work they do.

Because every person who works hard and honestly deserves utmost respect, regardless of their level in the hierarchy.

---

shopfloor, see the actual process, understand it, ask questions, and learn.

✓ **KEY TAKEAWAYS**

1. Don't focus only on top performer
2. Leverage personalities and skills for the good of the team
3. Learn how to delegate, do not micro-manage
4. Create a culture of Psychological Safety
5. Respect everybody as if they were your CEO

EMPATHIZE

Soft Skills

The second of the two letters **E** in the SERVE Model stands for **Empathize**. Empathy comes from the Greek ἐν (*in*) and -πάθεια (*suffering*), and refers to the capability to understand feelings and emotions of a person, usually without verbal communication.

When I decided to pursue an EMBA at Frankfurt School back in 2016, the main driver for my decision was my will to further develop my **soft skills**. With a Master's and a PhD in Engineering, I felt pretty solid on the technical side. On the soft-skills side, however, there were—let's say it gently—*opportunities for improvement*. As a matter of fact, soft skills are not the main focus in engineering schools, at least they were not 20 years ago. An EMBA Program was what I needed.

But what is meant with the term *soft skills*? Soft skills relate to how people work and interact with others, and include, but are not limited to, teamwork, networking, problem-solving, work ethic, conflict resolution, time management, creative thinking, empathy [Doyle, 2020].

> *"People will forget what you said, people will forget what you did, but people will never forget how you made them feel."*
> **Maya Angelou**, Poet & Civil Rights Activist

Empathy, in particular, is the one single skill—more than any other in my opinion—that differentiates a great boss, one you would go to war for, from a bad one, one you would leave today if you could.

Years ago, I went through a very painful divorce. The years between 2011 and 2014 have been the worst in my life. During those unpleasant days, I changed four supervisors. Two of them were on opposite ends of the empathy scale. When I shared with each of them my private struggle, the empathic supervisor offered me his support, comforted me with words and actions, reassured me that he and the team would have not left me alone. The non-empathic supervisor, on the other hand, was only concerned that the hell I was going through privately could slow down my performance at work. I still remember the few words he spoke one day, the words that *de facto* put an end to our relationship: "*I am sorry for what you are going through, but divorce is **your** problem, not mine*".

With the years, the emphatic supervisor became a mentor, a friend, a second father. Someone I still call for advice, several years after his retirement.

As for the non-empathic one, you can hardly imagine the party I gave after he announced his retirement...

Both supervisors had strong technical skills. What made the difference were their soft skills, empathy more than anything else.

"Companies Don't Succeed, People Do"[8]

Every single one of us, throughout life, faces times of suffering and pain. Severe diseases, loss of loved ones, divorces, financial troubles, natural disasters. Most people do not share their inner pain with others, especially not with their coworkers.

An empathic leader detects the pain in their eyes, in their faces, in their behavior. And tries to alleviate

---

[8] [Nelson, 2015]

it, by listening more than speaking, by acting more than promising, by caring instead of ignoring. An empathic leader can turn a work team into a second family, where members support each other whenever needed.

> *"If our inward griefs were seen written on our brow, how many would be pitied who are now envied!" ["Se a ciascun l'interno affanno si leggesse in fronte scritto, quanti mai, che invidia fanno, ci farebbero pietà"!]*
> **Pietro Metastasio**, Poet

Empathic leaders are crucial in departments like Human Resources, which are meant to focus on employees, their careers, their development, their growth. Too often I have witnessed **HR** managers focusing more on **H**eadcount **R**eduction (i.e., costs) than on their **H**uman **R**esources (i.e., employees), prioritizing shareholders over their own employees.

Shareholders are important, do not get me wrong, but are not *that* important. A company is, in its core, a group of employees working together. If they work together well, the company will succeed and be profitable, and shareholders will come and invest. If employees are neglected, mismanaged, humiliated, they will not work well, the company in the longer term will not be profitable, and shareholders will eventually invest their money somewhere else.

Team Building

Sharing inner pain comes naturally when teammates are also friends. It is unrealistic to expect each team member to become close friends with all other team members. However, even having just one or two friends in the team initiates the process of sharing information, discussing issues, asking for advice, which can alleviate the pain.

One effective way to accelerate the formation of friendships within a team is organizing **team-building events**.

Team-building events are activities aimed at engaging employees, enhancing social relations and improving team bonding [Scudamore, 2016]. Such events range from standard dinners to more creative group activities.

For a few years I was a member of a team which proved to be quite ingenious in its team-building events. Over the years, we practiced archery, went canoeing, played foot-basket, rode a Segway, climbed trees, drove *draisines* (pedal-powered rail-cycles), and went hiking in the forest. Obviously, team-building events need to be tailored to the demographics of the team in order to ensure that each and every team member feels included.

Team-building events contribute to generating in a team the spirit of **Ubuntu**, the South African philosophy of unity and collaboration made famous by Nelson Mandela [Gade, 2012], and often translated as "*I am because we are*". And the concept of *we* is at the core of highly successful teams: great leaders always think *we*, not *I*.

> *"There is a word in South Africa –*
> *Ubuntu – a word that captures*
> *Mandela's greatest gift: his recognition*
> *[...] that we achieve ourselves by*
> *sharing ourselves with others, and*
> *caring for those around us".*
> **Barack Obama**, Former US President

✓ KEY TAKEAWAYS

1. Focus on your Soft Skills, especially Empathy
2. Learn to detect inner pains, and help alleviating them
3. Employees are your most valuable resource
4. Promote Team-Building activities
5. Think we, not I

SERVE IN THE FAMILY

The Priority List

A couple of years ago, I attended a Manufacturing Engineering Leadership class. Among other assignments, participants were requested to read a book, *The Priority List* [Menasche, 2013].

Diagnosed with a terminal brain tumor, David Menasche, a high school English teacher, embarks in a 101-day, 8000-mile journey across the United States to visit his former students and see firsthand if and how he had made a difference in their lives. Heartbreaking and humorous at the same time, the book explores what each one of us wants and needs in life—love, family, friends, a job,...—, and forces readers to reflect and consider their own priority list.

The Priority List had a deep impact on me. Ever since I read Menasche's book, not only I reflected on my own priority list. I also encouraged people around me—EMBA classmates, coworkers, friends, even my own family members—to make *their* priority list. Such list works—sometimes unconsciously—as our inner compass, shows us what really matters to us and how we can make a positive difference for the people we care about. Once you have your own priority list, reflect on how much your daily actions are consistent with your list. Results may surprise you...

Obviously, different people will make different lists. Some will rank money as their top priority, others will prioritize love. Health will be on top for some, friendship for others. Family, in particular, seems to be in the Top-5 priorities of nearly every person I discussed the list with. It certainly is in my own Top-5.

> *"Never put your family, friends, or significant other low on your priority list. Prefer a handful of truly close friends to a hundred acquaintances."*
> **Sam Altman**, CEO of OpenAI

Universality of the SERVE Model

In the previous chapters we discussed how the SERVE Model can be applied in a business environment. However, the model is generic enough to be applicable in other contexts: a sports team, a political party, a group of friends, a family. Because Servant Leadership is rather a philosophy than a job title.

In the next sections we will focus on how the SERVE Model fits in a family environment, and how its five pillars—*Share*, *Encourage*, *Recognize*, *Value*, and *Empathize*—apply to family relations, especially those with spouse and children.

> *"They taught us at school that family is the most important thing for a human. Roma is my family. Have you ever heard of someone who left his poor parents to live with rich strangers?"*
> **Francesco Totti**, Former AS Roma Captain

Share

Lack of sharing is a recipe for trouble. Sharing, in a family context, mainly refers to open and honest communication, especially within the couple. Marriages start sinking when partners do not communicate, when they start hiding their feelings, their thoughts, their actions.

Similarly, lack of communication may lead to dramatic consequences when it takes place between children (especially teenagers) and their parents. Anorexia, bulimia, drinking problems, drugs are all signals of discomfort, often extreme cries of children who desperately ask their parents to be heard, understood, loved.

Open and honest sharing of problems, feelings, emotions can limit such phenomena, and foster an environment where active listening is often more important than talking, where the most relevant thing is hearing what is *not* said.

"Communication – the human connection – is the key to personal and career success."
Paul Meyer, Entrepreneur & Motivational Speaker

Encourage

I grew up in a family where knowledge and learning have always been encouraged and nurtured. My grandfather was a doctor and could speak seven languages, both my father and my mother were teachers. I grew up surrounded by books, and conversations on classes, students, tests, and grades were the norm at every meal.

School dropouts in the European Union are gradually decreasing, but are still as high as 10% of youngsters between 18 and 24 years old [Eurostat, 2020]. In other continents the situation is much worse: in Africa 42% of children leave school before the end of primary education [Unesco, 2012].

A learning culture with its roots in the family is key to encourage kids to learn today so they can encourage their own kids to learn tomorrow. As Mandela once said, "*education is the most powerful weapon* [...] *to change the world*". Ignorance nurtures racism, intolerance, extremism, and violence. Ignorant people are easier to control and manipulate.

> "*An investment in knowledge pays the best interest.*"
> **Benjamin Franklin**, Writer, Scientist & Diplomat

Recognize

When I was in college, my mother established a recognition ritual for me: every time I achieved an above-average grade in an exam, the two of us would have a nice meal together in my favorite restaurant.

I still keep wonderful memories of those days (and glorious meals...) and how appreciated and rewarded I felt. It was not the meal per se the main driver for me to do well and try to do even better the next time. It was the awareness that my mother was proud of me, that she was standing by my side and supporting me while I was building the necessary foundation for my future professional career. I doubt I would have done so well without parents appreciating and recognizing my efforts and my small victories.

I would like to highlight how my recognitions were meals with my mother. I have witnessed many parents celebrating their children's accomplishments with money or presents. My mother, however, was celebrating my accomplishments with moments together, she was building memories I still keep in my heart. I personally find time together way more rewarding than material gifts, because *money is not the main driver*. Not for me.

Recognizing our partner is equally important. Too often we take for granted what our spouse is doing for us, the love we receive. In the previous pages, we talked about the power of a Thank-You. Thanking, appreciating, rewarding our partner are fundamental actions to maintaining and reinforcing a long-lasting relationship.

> *"What's in your memory bank is far more important than what is in your bank."*
> **Karen Salmansohn**, Author & Designer

Value

Sometimes I have the feeling that school, especially elementary school, is the pitch where parents compete against each other.

Weekly schedules of first graders look as busy as those of c-suite executives: school until 4 or 5 pm, then time for homework, music lessons, sport activities, theater performance, parties with children's animation, church activities... you name it. Sometimes the only activity missing in such hectic schedules is what you would think should be the primary activity of a first grader: *playing*.

My point is that too often kids have to live with unreasonably high expectations from their parents. It is understandable that parents wish a better life for their children. Parents want for their kids opportunities they did not have in their own childhood. However, unreasonable expectations may generate stress, performance anxiety, and—when unmet—frustration and anger.

The SERVE Model assumes that each and every kid is a winner by birth. Servant parents help their kids grow their strengths, work on their weaknesses, and eventually find their own path in life. Servant parents support and encourage their children when they fail, and celebrate them when they succeed.

> *"Encourage and support your kids*
> *because children are apt to live up*
> *to what you believe of them."*
> **Lady Bird Johnson**, Former US First Lady

Empathize

Every one of us lives moments in life when it is extremely hard to find the strength and motivation to move on.

Even though such moments can affect any member of a family, this is especially true for teenagers who are struggling to find their role and place in the adult world. This is when they most need support and empathy from their parents. Children need to know that their parents are there for them, and always will, no matter what. A safe shelter with an open door, whenever a storm—*any* storm—comes.

> *"Pass along the value of empathy to our children [...] the ability to stand in somebody else's shoes; to look at the world through their eyes."*
> **Barack Obama**, Former US President

Communication between different generations is not easy. Never was, and never will be. Servant

Leadership, however, focuses on developing people—teenagers instead of employees in this case—to make them more autonomous, wiser, freer, and eventually more likely to become, one day, servant leaders themselves.

With the awareness that each one of us is a winner by birth, the servant leader, through empathy, can help develop a spirit of Ubuntu within his own family: *I am because we are.*

✓ KEY TAKEAWAYS

1. Reflect on your own Priority List
2. Foster open and honest communication
3. Education can change the world, encourage it!
4. Everlasting moments reward more than material gifts
5. Unreasonably high expectations are harmful
6. Make sure your kids see your door always open

CONCLUSIONS

As written in the INTRODUCTION, this book is about my personal vision of leadership, and is based on my own experience, both professional and private.

Leadership styles vary by person, and must also fit into the cultures of the organization and the geography where the team operates. I do not expect all the methods and approaches described in these pages to be adopted by each and every team leader. Feel free to select the ones which fit best your leadership style, your company and your geographic location.

The SERVE Model is a roadmap meant to inspire, not a set of laws to diligently obey. The model is universal enough to be applicable outside of the business environment, as we discussed in the previous chapter.

Before we write the word *END* to this book, there is one more story I would like to share with you. I heard it years ago from my supervisor at the time. The name of the story is *The Star Thrower* [Eiseley, 1979][9].

---

[9] https://www.youtube.com/watch?v=Z-aVMdJ3Aok.

"[...] there was a human boy walking along a beach. There had just been a storm, and starfish had been scattered along the sands. The boy knew the fish would die, so he began to fling the fish to the sea. But every time he threw a starfish, another would wash ashore. An old [man] saw what the child was doing. He called out, 'Boy, what are you doing?'. 'Saving the starfish!' replied the boy. 'But your attempts are useless, child! Every time you save one, another one returns, often the same one! You can't save them all, so why bother trying? Why does it matter, anyway?' called the old man. The boy thought about this for a while, a starfish in his hand; he answered, 'Well, it matters to this one'. And then he flung the starfish into the welcoming sea."

The point I would like to make here is that each one of us can—*does*—impact those around us: coworkers, friends, family, pets, ... starfish. It is up to us to decide what kind of impact we want to make, what legacy we want to leave behind us, how we want to be remembered once we will be gone.

Stephen Covey in his book *The 7 Habits of Highly Effective People* [Covey, 1989] talks about the words each one of us would like to hear spoken at our own funeral. I prefer to picture a more positive scene, and think at how former coworkers will talk about me while I will be enjoying retirement on a sunny Italian beach, with an ice-cold glass of *Frascati* wine in my hand. The idea, though, is the same: what impact have we made?

The boy in the story made a positive difference for the starfish he managed to fling back into the sea. The SERVE model shows how to make a positive difference by **S**haring, **E**ncouraging, **R**ecognizing, **V**aluing and **E**mpathizing with the people around us, both at work and in the family.

A servant leader can motivate people to go the extra mile and achieve results far exceeding expectations, can improve their thinking without telling them what to do [Rock, 2006].

I always aspire—and will continue doing so—to make a positive difference for my team members, my family, my friends. I hope that what you read in this book helps *you* make a positive difference in everything *you* do.

> *"What we do in life echoes in eternity."*
> **Russel Crowe**, Actor (in the movie *Gladiator*)

ABOUT THE AUTHOR

Dr. Marco Lemessi holds a Master's and a PhD in Engineering from the University of Rome *La Sapienza*, and an Executive MBA from Frankfurt School of Finance & Management.

In the business since 1998, Dr. Lemessi has spoken at tens of international conferences and events in Europe, America, Africa, and Asia, mainly on topics related to Discrete-Event Simulation, Simulation-Based Optimization, Data Analytics, and Machine Learning.

Native of Rome, Italy, Dr. Lemessi started his career as a consultant and lecturer at the Universities of Rome and Perugia. Later, he lived and worked in the United States prior to relocating to Germany, where he still lives.

In addition to being an engineer and a team leader, he is the proud father of a ten-year-old girl, Elena, an avid reader, and a passionate world traveler.

SERVE to lead is his first non-fiction book after the sci-fi novel *CHANGING HISTORY* on time travel and Roman history, published in July 2020.

Follow Dr. Lemessi on Social Media:

LinkedIn: www.linkedin.com/in/marcolemessi/

Xing: www.xing.com/profile/Marco_Lemessi/cv

REFERENCES

Arets J., Jennings C., Heijnen V. – *70:20:10 into action* – https://702010institute.com/wp-content/uploads/2018/11/Primer-702010-into-action.pdf, 2016.

Beedle M. – *SCRUM is an Organization Pattern* – http://www.jeffsutherland.org/objwld98/scrum_pattern.html, 1997.

Blanchard K., Oncken W. Jr & Burrows H. – *The One Minute Manager meets the Monkey* – HarperCollins, 1990.

Covey S. – *The 7 Habits of Highly Effective People* – Simon & Schuster, 1989.

DeakinCo. – *Developing world-class employees with the 70:20:10 model* – https://www.deakinco.com/media-centre/news/Developing-world-class-employees-with-the-70:20:10-model, 2018.

Doyle A. – *What Are Soft Skills? Definition and Examples of Soft Skills* – https://www.thebalancecareers.com/what-are-soft-skills-2060852, 2020.

Edmondson A. – *Psychological Safety and Learning Behavior in Work Teams* – Johnson Graduate School of Management, Cornell University, 1999.

Eiseley L. – *The Star Thrower* – Mariner Books, 1979.

Eurostat – *Early leavers from education and training* – https://ec.europa.eu/eurostat/statistics-explained/index.php/Early_leavers_from_education_and_training, 2020.

Friedman J. – *Pronoun Problems: "He/She", "He or She", or Just Plain "He"?* – https://www.writersdigest.com/write-better-fiction/pronoun-problems-heshe-he-or-she-or-just-plain-he, 2010.

Gade C. – *What is Ubuntu? Different Interpretations among South Africans of African Descent* – South African Journal of Philosophy, 2012.

geekbot - *Daily Standup Meetings: Everything You Need to Know (Standup Agenda, Purpose, Common Pitfalls, and More!)* – https://geekbot.com/blog/daily-standup-meeting/, 2020.

Goleman D. – *Emotional Intelligence – Why it can matter more than IQ* – Bantam Books, 1995.

Greenleaf R. – *The servant as leader* – The Robert K. Greenleaf Center, 1970.

Harari Y. – *Homo Deus – A Brief History of Tomorrow* – HarperCollins, 2017.

Kaplan R., Norton D. – *The Balanced Scorecard – Measures that Drive Performance* – Harvard Business Review, 1992.

Kelly K. – *The Inevitable: Understanding the 12 Technological Forces that will Shape our Future* – Penguin Books, 2016.

Kohn A. – *Why Incentive Plans Cannot Work* – Harvard Business Review, 1993.

Kotter J. – *Leading Change* – Harvard Business Review, 2012.

Maniccia G. – *Approcci di Leadership* – IFAP, Istituto per la Formazione e l'Aggiornamento Professionale, 1993.

Menasche D. – *The Priority List* – Simon & Schuster, Inc., 2013.

Nelson B. – *Companies Don't Succeed, People Do* – Sourcebooks, Inc., 2015.

Rahrovani Y., Pinsonneault A., Austin R. – *If You Cut Employees Some Slack, Will They Innovate?* – MIT Sloan Management Review, https://sloanreview.mit.edu/article/if-you-cut-employees-some-slack-will-they-innovate/, 2018.

Robert K. Greenleaf Center [RKGC] for Servant Leadership – *The Servant as Leader* – https://www.greenleaf.org/what-is-servant-leadership/, 2021.

Rock D. – *Quiet Leadership – Help People Think Better, Don't Tell Them What to Do!* – Collins, 2006.

Scudamore B. – *Why Team Building Is The Most Important Investment You'll Make* – https://www.forbes.com/sites/brianscudamore/2016/03/09/why-team-building-is-the-most-important-investment-youll-make, 2016.

Torrington D., Hall L., Taylor S., Atkinson C. – *Human Resource Management (9th Edition)* – Pearson, 2014.

Unesco - *42% of African school children will drop out before the end of primary education* – http://www.unesco.org/new/en/member-states/single-view/news/42_of_african_school_children_will_drop_out_before_the_end*, 2012.

Womack J. – *Gemba Walks* – Lean Enterprise Institute, Inc., 2011.

Zaleznik A. – *Managers and Leaders: Are They Different?* – https://hbr.org/2004/01/managers-and-leaders-are-they-different, 2004.

Made in the USA
Las Vegas, NV
25 February 2021